How to Build Confidence and Stand Up for Yourself:

Firmly tell anyone bothering you: "Stop!"

Set new rules together as a group!

Make a hasty retreat!

Say no!

Invite others to play different competitive games that are fun for everyone!

Tell someone if you yourself are angry!

Shout!

Sing power songs!

Be strong like a lion, eagle, or bear!

Pretend those bothering you are invisible!

Team up with others!

Have a chest full of treasures with you!

Ask someone for help directly!

If you are angry, get your rage out safely!

Tell those bothering you that they are unfair, cowardly, and mean.

Find a unique treasure within yourself and hold onto it!

Sky Pony Press books may be purchased in bulk at special discounts for sales promotion, corporate gifts, fund-raising, or educational purposes. Special editions can also be created to specifications. For details, contact the Special Sales Department, Sky Pony Press, 307 West 36th Street, 11th Floor, New York, NY 10018 or info@skyhorsepublishing.com.
Sky Pony® is a registered trademark of Skyhorse Publishing, Inc.®, a Delaware corporation.
Visit our website at www.skyponypress.com.

10 9 8 7 6 5 4 3 2 1

Manufactured in China, June 2019
This product conforms to CPSIA 2008

Library of Congress Cataloging-in-Publication Data is available on file.

Cover provided by Loewe Verlag GmbH
Cover illustration by Dagmar Geisler

Print ISBN: 978-1-5107-4651-0
Ebook ISBN: 978-1-5107-4662-6

I Can Build Confidence

Written by
Elisabeth Zöller

Illustrated by
Dagmar Geisler

Translated by
Andrea Jones Berasaluce

Sky Pony Press
New York

Today, Kim cannot wait to get to kindergarten. That's because she has a new backpack that she wants everyone to see! When she wears her new backpack, she feels big—almost as big as a first grader!

Two kids block her path. Kim stands still. She holds her breath. Hopefully today they won't do anything to her. She knows both kids: big Grit and nasty Fritz from her class.

They don't like Kim. They're always mean to her. It has been like this the whole year. Because they're bigger than the others in class, they've been showing off, acting as if they're the greatest. They both want to decide everything for everyone in kindergarten.

And whenever the kindergarten teachers aren't looking, they bother all the other children.

"Please let me go by," Kim says. Her heart pounds. She takes a step forward.

But Grit and Fritz just stop and grin hideously.

"I've done nothing to you," Kim says softly. She looks around for a moment. But no one else is walking to school this way. With someone else, she could easily get by.

"Please! Let me through," whispers Kim.

"Please, please, let me through!" Grit mimics Kim and laughs.

"The school shouldn't let babies in so easily," says Fritz. "Give us your backpack! Then you can pass."

Kim gulps. "I'll tell Ms. Blume," she mumbles.

"What? You big baby, you wouldn't dare! If you snitch, we'll hit you!" Fritz waves his fist.

And Kim shrinks.

"Baby, baby!" shouts Grit.

Kim can't listen anymore.

Fritz pushes her, and Kim nearly falls.

She becomes smaller and smaller. Tiny, like a little mouse that cannot even squeak.

And then, someone is coming. Loud steps. Getting closer.

Kim would like to crawl into a mouse hole and hide.

She doesn't realize that Grit and Fritz have disappeared, fast like lightning.

She crouches on the ground and cries.

The steps suddenly stop in front of her.

"Help!" Kim wants to yell. "Help!"

But she doesn't make a sound.

"Hello," says a voice.

Cautiously Kim looks up. There's an older boy standing in front of her.

He's at least twelve years old. Will he also do something to her?

"What's wrong?" the boy asks.

No, he doesn't want to do anything to her . . . right?

"Nothing," Kim says, quickly wiping away her tears.

She feels a little ashamed.

"But why are you crying? Were those two kids bothering you?"

Kim shakes her head. She cannot say anything.

"Hm . . . come on, stand up," says the boy.

Kim realizes that her knees are still shaky.

"Is everything really alright? Or did they do something to you?" asks the older boy.

Kim shakes her head again. She won't let out even a peep, otherwise she really would be a snitch.

"It's nothing!" Kim says quickly. "I have to go to kindergarten now." She waves to the nice boy and leaves.

Ms. Blume, the kindergarten teacher, welcomes Kim. She even gives her a little hug hello.

That makes Kim feel better. But Kim doesn't want to tell her anything.

"What a great backpack! You sure look forward to school!" says Ms. Blume.

Kim nods and takes off her backpack. Her classmates surround her, and Kim is allowed to show off her backpack. She likes this. Yes, she always looks forward to school. She is a big schoolgirl now. And nobody can do anything to her anymore.

But here come big Grit and nasty Fritz. They jostle Kim between them. "Baby, baby!"

The other children hide. Kim is alone with her new backpack.

The two of them remain next to her. Very close. Kim can barely breathe.

Nasty Fritz whispers in her ear: "Baby!"

Kim becomes ever smaller.

Then Ms. Blume calls all the children together.

Fritz and Grit disappear to the other corner of the room.

Kim sighs in relief.

Ms. Blume spreads many large white shoe boxes out on the floor.

"Today everyone is making their own treasure chest," explains Ms. Blume. "Each person has many treasures inside. One can sing, another can paint wonderfully, a third can make crafts. We just have to discover these treasures. And as long as you want to keep the treasures from your chest just to yourself, you shut the lid.

It takes time to want to show one's treasures, because many laugh at others' treasures and talents."

"Oh, yes," Kim thinks.

"But if you want to show them off, keep your treasure chest open so everyone can see."

"Great!" the kids shout. "When do we start?"

"Should we paint or make crafts or sing songs?"

"Whatever you want," says Ms. Blume. "Everybody does it the way they want to. Every person has many treasures buried deep inside."

"Where are the treasures then?" asks Kim.

"Are the treasures in my stomach?" Kai giggles.

"Or in my ears?"

"In my big loose tooth?"

"Perhaps," replies Ms. Blume. "It's different for everyone. But when you reach deep inside of you, you'll feel where you've stored all your treasures."

"Mine are in my feet." Paul has understood: He is a soccer player. He knows he can score goals. Paul's strengths are soccer and running.

Kati's strength is singing. Luis's strength is words. Philipp's strength is numbers.

"The treasures can be everywhere," says Ms. Blume, "In your head, in your thoughts, in your dreams, in your stomach, in your arms, legs, and feet."

"And so you don't lose them, put into your very own treasure chest a picture, a craft, or something that reminds you of your treasures. Sometimes a song can also remind you of your treasures."

Ms. Blume picks up her guitar and sings a song: "The Treasure Song," about how everyone is strong. Curiously, the students all listen. Soon they clap, stomp, drum, and sing along.

Everyone has a treasure vast,
and up we dig it—lightning fast.

When hurt, to feel small you're made,
sad, alone, and afraid.
Come to us, come over here.
Becoming invincible's easy, it's clear.

Everyone has a treasure vast,
and up we dig it—lightning fast.

You tell Fear: "Now away with you!
I'm strong as a bear and a bull, too."
From a tub full of anger, it shows,
that slowly a new courage grows.

Everyone has a treasure vast,
and up we dig it—lightning fast.

With my treasures inside, well I'll be,
I like myself just as me!

Look, I'm going to grow up.
I'm strong now—excellent, yup.

Everyone has a treasure vast,
and up we dig it—lightning fast.

And finally, Ms. Blume says proudly: "You are all wonderful treasures, children!"

"That's really great!" Kim thinks. "I'm a wonderful treasure." And she already has an idea what her treasure is.

Everyone runs to get started! They'll find treasures, dig them up, paint and make crafts.

They sing together rambunctiously as they work:

"Everyone has a treasure vast, and up we dig it—lightning fast." They are so excited!

Suddenly, when Ms. Blume isn't looking, Fritz steps on Kim's treasure chest. And Grit chops the chest from behind with a paintbrush.

The two grin meanly.

They've left a real hole in Kim's treasure chest.

Kim wants to cry out in anger.

She would love to crawl into a cozy corner now. Forever. Or at least until Grit and Fritz finally leave her alone.

She bites her lip to keep from crying.

"I'm still a treasure!" she thinks. "I'm strong, too!"

Kim takes her brush, gradually dips it into water, rinses it out carefully. She first breathes slowly and deeply, then breathes and counts very slowly to ten.

She stands tall, feet planted in front of Grit and Fritz, and asks: "Can't you do anything besides bother us, be nasty, and break things?"

Grit looks at Fritz. Fritz looks at Grit. They are no longer smiling.

They disappear to the corner without saying anything mean.

Kim's eyes grow wide. She hadn't expected this to happen.

She is still very excited. It's as though inside her courage and her fear are chasing each other wildly.

"We can glue the hole closed again," Ms. Blume says consolingly to Kim.

But Kim turns around and says, "The hole stays. That's the meanness. It stays. It cannot be changed. But me, I can make myself strong."

"Great," says Ms. Blume, "that's even better. Yes, you can make yourself strong!" And she says a little louder: "And I'll talk to Fritz and Grit later. They can certainly be strong too without bullying others!"

Kim paints her treasures in peace.

Then she closes her treasure chest tight.

She hums to herself: "With my treasures inside, well I'll be, I like myself just as me!"

She can't wait to get home. She has such a wonderful treasure chest.

Maybe she'll let Mom and Dad look inside.

They'll be amazed. "With my treasures inside, well I'll be, I like myself just as me! I am a wonderful treasure!

And soon a first grader, too. I am so big and strong!"

About the Authors

Elisabeth Zöller was born in Brilon in 1945 and studied German, pedagogy, art history, and French in Munich, Lausanne, and Münster. Then she worked as a high school teacher for many years before she became a freelance writer in 1989 and made a name for herself chiefly with books against violence. Her great concern is non-violent learning and coexistence—therefore, she is engaged in teacher training, parent nights, and readings and lessons for children and adolescents. She lives with her husband in Münster.

Dagmar Geisler is a German author and illustrator. She studied graphic design at the University of Applied Sciences in Wiesbaden and worked for several publishing houses and broadcasting companies. Today, Dagmar focuses mainly on children's books, both as an illustrator and an author. She illustrated *My Body Belongs to Me from My Head to My Toes* which received the Silver Feather (Silberne Feder) Children's Book Prize from the German Medical Women's Association, and is the illustrator of *My Feelings and Me.* She lives with her family in Munich, Germany.

How to Build Confidence and Stand Up for Yourself:

Firmly tell anyone bothering you: "Stop!"

Shout!

Say no!

Ask someone for help directly!

Be strong like a lion, eagle, or bear!

Take a treasure everywhere, for example, a horse chestnut, that shows you how you can be: because the outside is a bit prickly, you can protect yourself from others. And under the prickly shell, it is very soft and fluffy—that is you, as something very precious, special, vulnerable. But then inside is the hard pit, to which you can always hold, it always remains, even if the precious, soft part should get a bit scratched.

Pretend those bothering you are invisible!

Team up with others!

Have a chest full of treasures with you!

Tell those bothering you that they are unfair, cowardly, and mean.

Sing power songs!

If you yourself are angry, get your rage out safely!

Make a hasty retreat!

Find a unique treasure within yourself and hold onto it!